ESTHER
The God Who Is Silent
Is Still Sovereign

ESTHER

THE GOD WHO IS SILENT
IS STILL SOVEREIGN

NORMAN DE JONG

A REFORMED FELLOWSHIP BIBLE STUDY

Reformed Fellowship Inc.
www.reformedfellowship.net

Esther. The God Who Is Silent Is Still Sovereign

©2018 by Norman De Jong

All rights reserved. No part of this book may be reproduced or transmitted in any form or by any means whatsoever without the prior written permission of the publisher, except in the case of brief quotations embodied in critical articles and reviews. Please refer all pertinent questions to the publisher:

Reformed Fellowship, Inc.
(877) 532–8510
president@reformedfellowship.net

Unless otherwise indicated, all Scripture quotations are from the Reformation Study Bible, English Standard Version, published by Ligonier Ministries and edited by R. C. Sproul, 2008. Used by permission. All rights reserved.

Book design by Jeff Steenholdt

ISBN 978-1-935369-15-8

*Dedicated to the hundreds of
persons who have joined me in Bible
studies over the past twenty years,
encouraging them to drink deeply
from the Word of God.*

Contents

Introduction **9**

1. Conspicuous Consumption or Ostentatious Display? **19**
2. A Jewish Orphan Becomes the New Queen **27**
3. The Seed of Warfare Are Being Sown **35**
4. Confusion, Crying, and Chaos **43**
5. From Feasting to Fasting to Feasting **51**
6. The Turning of the Tide **59**
7. Radical Transformations **67**
8. An Unbalanced Civil War **75**

Introduction

Some people claim to "love" the book of Esther. It excites them. It tells them about a beautiful woman named Esther who becomes queen of Persia. The story contains conflict, it contains romance, it contains royalty. For some, it satisfies their desire for feminist revenge. For others, it puts a stamp of approval on beauty pageants. If such are our motivations, we are barking up the wrong tree.

The book of Esther is unique in a number of ways. It has been the object of much controversy, even though it is loved and treasured by the Jewish community. For many Christians, it is an enigma because it never mentions the name of God. Superficially, it seems as though God is missing from the story. Also, it recounts violent, widespread revenge by the Jews against their enemies, which seems to contradict the biblical message that vengeance belongs to God and not to man. Furthermore, there is a secular tone to the book, highlighting beauty pageants and sexual promiscuity that should be repugnant to Bible believers. Writing a commentary on the book of Esther presents an unusual challenge. In order for us to understand the book of Esther, we will need to recognize several important truths.

Important Preconceptions

■ **First and foremost, the book of Esther is an accepted part of the Old Testament canon.** It is, therefore, the Word of God. It must be treated as God's revelation or disclosure to his Body, the church. It is, therefore, infallible and authoritative. Some commentaries will dispute that claim and argue that this book should not be in the Bible. It never mentions the name of God and, seemingly, does not point to Jesus Christ.

■ **Second, Esther is primarily a historical book.** It describes for us events that occurred sometime in history. It is imperative, then, that we know when those events occurred. If we assume that the Old Testament is organized in historical sequence, we will conclude or assume that the events of Esther occurred sometime after the events in Ezra and Nehemiah. The Old Testament, after all, has the book of Esther following Ezra and Nehemiah but well before the books of Psalms or Isaiah or Daniel.

■ **All human beings operate with certain assumptions or basic beliefs as we live our lives.** Without critical examination, we accept some statements or implied assertions as being true and worthy of acceptance. When we do that uncritically, we call them "presumptions" or "preconceptions" or "assumptions." As serious students of God's Holy Word, it is important that our assumptions are based on facts and not on opinions, for **opinions can easily be in error. Our preconceptions have to conform to reality.**

■ **The Bible is rightly described as "historical, progressive revelation."** That means that it informs us about real historical events that occurred over periods of time. These events did not all occur at one specific time or point in history but over many decades, centuries, and millennia. God has progressively revealed his plan of salvation and the knowledge of himself so that we could know him truthfully and live accordingly. We should **also add the descriptive word "literary" to that definition because the Bible is a book.** It has all the qualities of literature, which, understood correctly, will enhance our understanding of the Bible and our appreciation for it.

■ **Events have consequences which follow after the events and do not precede them.** One of the qualities of God's Holy Word is that it frequently contains specific timelines and dates for events. The book of Esther, for example, begins with the phrase "Now in the days of Ahasuerus, . . . in the third year of his reign" (Esther 1:1, 3). What year was that? When did that occur? Working backwards in our Bibles, we read, "Now it happened in the month of Chislev, in the twentieth year, as I was in Susa" (Neh. 1:1). When we jump ahead to the book of Daniel, we read there that "in the third year of the reign of Jehoikim, . . . Nebuchadnezzar" (Dan. 1:1). Throughout these historical books there are frequent, specific dates or times mentioned. We need to pay careful attention to those so that we understand correct chronological sequencing. An event that occurred in 605 BC is going to influence or affect people's lives and events in subsequent years. A proclamation given in 539 BC, for example, is going to impact the lives of people living in 538 BC but not those living in 544 BC.

■ **God is sovereign ruler over men and nations, as is clearly taught in the book of Daniel.** The sovereignty of God is the primary theme in the book of Daniel. It is demonstrated in a variety of ways, among which are examples of God using pagan persons to accomplish his divine purposes and objectives. God often draws straight lines with crooked sticks. We have to assume that this principle is also operative in the book of Esther. Even though God is not specifically mentioned in the book of Esther, we can be sure that God is directing and controlling all the persons and events that are described. God is spirit, so we cannot see him with the naked eye, but we can see him with the eye of faith.

■ **God often uses fallible human beings to accomplish his purposes.** For example, Jeremiah refers to Nebuchadnezzar as "my servant" (Jer. 27:6). God has also described King Cyrus of Persia as "my shepherd" and my "anointed" (Isa. 44:28; 45:1), even though Cyrus did not know him (Isa. 45:4–5). As we peruse the books of Ezra and Nehemiah, we see King Artaxerxes of Persia issuing specific commands to advance the kingdom of God, even though the text leaves his personal relationship to Christ in doubt. God controls and uses those whom he chooses to carry out his plans, even though these people are obviously evil and responsible for their wicked actions.

Given these regulative principles, we will need to construct an accurate time line of events if we are to see how these events might possibly affect those persons that follow after them. As we construct such a chronology, we will be able to understand how earlier events might affect later events.

As we thumb through our English Bibles, we find four historical books that deal with events in the Persian Empire. In order of appearance, they are the books of Ezra, Nehemiah, Esther, and Daniel. If you have been following our Bible studies during the last years, you will recall that we have recently finished studies of Ezra and Nehemiah. Our study over these next months will focus on the book of Esther. Since the Old Testament begins with Genesis and moves through a number of historical books, most of us assume that these four are in correct chronological sequence. Of the four, Daniel tends to generate a lot of interest because it contains events and miracles that fascinate us. Daniel is also full of pictures of the pre-incarnate Christ, making it one of the most messianic books of the Old Testament. Daniel is full of Sunday school lessons, but we tend to focus only on the first six chapters. We tend to find the last half of that book to be somewhat confusing and difficult to understand. When we realize that much of that is prophetic and is rooted in the Persian Empire, we have added reason to avoid that section.

Typical pastors and professors know very little about the Persian Empire because that subject seldom gets studied by Reformed theologians. Most of our seminaries in the Western world do not teach courses on Persian history or culture. Since Ezra, Nehemiah, and Esther are set in the Persian Empire, we tend to ignore what we don't know. In fact, most laypeople assume that those last three books are in correct chronological order, with Esther being the latest book and the latest person of the four. That is a wrong assumption, as any serious study of chronology will indicate.

The Biblical Sequence	The Chronological Sequence
Ezra	Daniel
Nehemiah	Esther
Esther	Ezra
Daniel	Nehemiah

The Chronology of Esther (All dates are BC, before Christ)

740–701	The prophet Isaiah foretells the destruction of Israel and the coming of Cyrus, King of Persia (see Isa. 44:24–45:13)
605	Nebuchadnezzar begins siege of Jerusalem; Daniel and friends carried into captivity (2 Kings 24:10–16; Jer. 52:4–11; Dan. 1:1–2)
586	Jerusalem and the temple are destroyed (2 Kings 25:8–10; Jer. 52:12–16; Ezek. 9:1–11)
539	The Medes and the Persians conquer Babylon and kill Belshazzar; Darius and Cyrus become co-rulers over the Medo-Persian Empire (Dan. 5:30; 6:28)
538	King Cyrus issues his edict, allowing the Jews to return to Jerusalem and Judah; fifty thousand people respond and go back to Judea (Ezra 1:1; 6:3; 2 Chron. 36:22)
536	Work on the temple begins, is opposed, but continues (Ezra 1—4)
530–522	Cambyses (aka Ahasuerus) is king of Persia (Ezra 4:6)
530	Work on the temple is stopped by force of arms (Ezra 4:6, 23)
522–486	Darius I reigns over Persia (Ezra 5)
520	Work on the temple resumes (Ezra 5)
515	The temple is completed and dedicated (Ezra 6:15–18)

494–449	The Persians wage war against the Greeks and the Egyptians
486–465	Xerxes (aka Ahasuerus) reigns over Persian Empire (Ezra 4:6; Esther 1:1)
483	Vashti is deposed as queen (Esther 1:3)
479	Esther becomes queen of Persia (Esther 2:16)
465–424	Artaxerxes I becomes king and reigns over Persia (Ezra 4:7; 7:11)
458	Ezra is commissioned by Artaxerxes to go to Jerusalem and teach the law of God (Ezra 7:7)
445	Nehemiah is commissioned by Artaxerxes to go to Jerusalem and repair the walls of the city and to repopulate the city (Neh. 2:1); he governs for twelve years
445	The walls are finished in fifty-two days (Neh. 6:15); the city is restored

[Handwritten annotations: "Ruled over 127 Provinces"; "Xerxes reigned 19 yrs"; "4 yrs after Vashti"; "First group to Jerusalem"; "Second group"]

If we operate with the assumption that Ezra and Nehemiah occur before Esther, we will almost certainly make a number of serious mistakes. Notice, too, that Daniel appears much later in our Bibles but predates the other three. Daniel is a very old man by the time that Darius, one of the Persian kings, puts him in the lions' den (Dan. 6). The Lord shuts the mouths of the lions. King Darius is mightily impressed. Notice also that this Persian king then issues a decree for all the people within his dominion to "tremble and fear before the God of Daniel for he is the living God" (Dan. 6:26–27).

That decree is issued in 538 BC, fifty-nine years before Esther becomes queen. When we backtrack into the book of Daniel, we note there that Nebuchadnezzar has also issued some potent proclamations, insisting that Jehovah is the true God and the one to worship (Dan. 2:47; 3:28–29; 4:34–37). This latter proclamation is directed to "all peoples, nations, and languages, that dwell in all the earth" (Dan. 4:1). All the residents of the Babylonian Empire are commanded by their king to worship the God of the Bible. A few years later all the residents in the Persian Empire are also commanded by their king to worship the God of the Bible, known then as the God of the Jews. The powers of both of those empires are behind those commands. There are many idol worshippers throughout the empire who find this command to be repugnant. Such religious persuasion is almost ground for revolt.

As we peruse this chronology, note first that Daniel and his friends are taken captive to Babylon in the year 605 BC. Notice next the date for Esther becoming queen (479 BC), which is four years after Vashti has been deposed. What transpired during the interval? Compare those events with the appearance of Ezra (458 BC) and Nehemiah (445 BC). Notice, too, that Haman's effort to exterminate all the Jews in the entire Persian Empire would have produced major consequences. Humanly speaking, if all the Jews had been killed, Ezra and Nehemiah could never have been commissioned by King Artaxerxes to lead worship in Jerusalem or restore the walls and the city. Our Bibles, humanly speaking, would not have the books of Esther, Ezra, Nehemiah, or Malachi, since all the Jews would have been annihilated by their enemies. The prevention of that planned genocide is then an event of monumental significance. Of even greater importance is the fact that all of Christ's genealogy would have been cut off. Esther is, therefore, very important in the development of historical, redemptive theology. Please join me in praying frequently for wisdom and insight.

Discussion Starters

1. Did you assume that the story of Esther followed after the stories of Ezra and Nehemiah? Is it difficult to adjust your thinking to the chronology offered here? Why?

2. Did you assume that Esther became queen soon after Vashti was deposed? What happened during those four years between the two events?

3. Are secular historians to be trusted? Are secular historians biased and prejudiced? What important factor are they ignoring? How significant is that? *The development of historical redemptive theology*

4. On December 7, 1941, the Japanese attacked Pearl Harbor. What effects did that attack have on world history?

5. In 539 BC King Cyrus of Persia issued a proclamation allowing Jewish captives to return to Jerusalem and Judah. He also granted them extensive privileges and immense wealth (Ezra 1:1–11; 2:64–70). What effect might this proclamation have had on all the idolaters in the empire?

6. Are human beings inclined by nature to love God and to obey his laws (see Rom. 3:9–18)? What types of response might we expect when kings issue decrees demanding worship of the true God?

7. If you were living during Daniel's time, what would be your reaction to the commands issued by King Darius? Would you expect widespread compliance?

8. If you were an idol worshiper, what would be your reaction to these same commands?

Chapter 1

Conspicuous Consumption or Ostentatious Display?

Scripture: Esther 1

As we begin reading in the book of Esther, we notice immediately that we are being introduced to one of the kings of the Persian Empire, Ahasuerus by name. We note, too, that he is only "in the third year of his reign" (1: 3), suggesting that he may be a relatively young monarch. Furthermore, we are told that his empire is very large, extending all the way from the Indus River in India to the country of Ethiopia in northern Africa and to the Greek cities in eastern Europe. This vast expanse of land is divided into 127 provinces, or legislative districts, somewhat akin to our states or counties. This is the largest empire in the then-known world. The emperor is then an important world power figure.

This king is best known by the name of Xerxes, given to him by the Greek historians who recorded the wars between the Greeks and the Persians from 490 to 470 BC. These Persian wars were initiated by the Persians under Darius II, who ruled from 522 to 486 BC. Darius developed a huge military force of both soldiers and naval vessels, enough to challenge the Greek city-states of Athens and Sparta.[1] The Persians were able to spread waves of destruction on the cities of Greece but were not able to win any major battles. A decisive battle occurred at Marathon in 490 BC, preventing the Persian army from attacking Athens. After five years of extended and intense conflict, the Persian military had to withdraw in disgrace.

In 486 BC Darius II died, and his son, Ahasuerus (Xerxes), became king of Persia. This is the royal monarch we meet on the pages of Esther. In the Western literary tradition, Xerxes is a synonym for arrogance, despotism, and impiety. According to the Greek historian Herodotus, Xerxes "devoted himself to gathering the whole available strength of the Empire with a view to overwhelming Greece by the force of numbers."[2] According to this same historian, Xerxes vowed "to march an army through Europe against Greece . . . and would not rest until I have taken and burnt Athens. . . . We shall make the Persian territory co-extensive with the air of heaven . . . and will make them all one territory, marching through the whole of Europe."[3] In his inaugural speech, Xerxes declared "that we may at once acquire an increase in glory and . . . [become] even more productive than we now possess."[4] Xerxes apparently had some grandiose plans for the expansion of his empire, attempting to enlarge it well beyond the 127 provinces that his father had organized. In 481 BC he again attempted a major campaign against Greece, hoping to fulfill his pledge. According to Professor Lee, this expedition ended in failure at both Thermopylae in 480 BC and at Salamis in 479 BC.[5] Those defeats brought him back to Susa, bent but not broken.

The writer of Esther seemingly has no interest in this military side of the story but focuses solely on events within Susa, the capital of Persia, one thousand miles away from the fields of battle. Quite probably, he (or she) knew about these wars but chose to ignore them and shine the spotlight on a huge celebration within the capital. Whoever is writing this account is well acquainted with the character and culture of this extensive empire. The writer never identifies himself in the book, leaving scholars the task of trying to identify whom this might be. Judging from the content of the story, it almost certainly is neither Esther nor Mordecai, even though they are the book's central characters. It is very probably a knowledgeable Jew who understood the laws and practices of Persian culture. Because the book is openly and avowedly pro-Jewish and is being used as a promotion for the Feast of Purim, it probably is a historian or scribe living during the fifth century (499–400 BC) within the confines of the empire, and, probably, within the capital city. The author knows the names and duties of many top officials in the king's inner circle. Linguistic critics have noted that the writing style of Esther is very similar to that of the books of First and Second Chronicles, giving us another clue as to probable author. Saint Augustine concluded that the author was Ezra, who is described as "a scribe skilled in the law of Moses" (Ezra 7:6). My own observations would lead me to conclude that Augustine is probably correct, but our analysis does not hinge on that.

What we have in the opening chapter of this book is a description of a lavish, extended exercise in self-aggrandizement. This demonstration continues for 180 days, or one half of a year. The text tells us that the purpose of this was to "show the riches of his royal glory and the splendor and pomp of his greatness for many days" (1:4). This kind of exercise reminds me of the lengthy demonstrations of military might carried out occasionally by the president of China and by Putin in Russia. Today we also see that kind of pompous parading by Kim Jong Il in North Korea. Like those despots, King Ahasuerus is impressed with his own greatness and wants the whole empire to participate in this display.

He has the markings of a megalomaniac, in love with himself and worshipping his own successes. As commanding officer of the army and navy, he can claim only limited military success, having put down rebellions in Egypt and in Babylon. But those minor victories do not prevent him from blowing his own horn. Returning to Susa, he has marshaled the army of Persia and Media, along with the nobles and governors of the provinces, to assemble in the empire's capital city, Susa. This prolonged celebration, in sociological language, is ostentatious display. Everyone who is anyone is expected to make the journey, even if it meant traveling from Egypt or India or Macedonia. It is intended to motivate the empire for his planned invasion of Greece and the burning of Athens. Come to observe our greatness and anticipate glorious victory!

This celebration in Susa reminds us of a similar display of self-centered importance conducted by King Nebuchadnezzar, recorded for us in Daniel 4:28–34. The difference between these two events is that God cautioned Nebuchadnezzar through a dream and through some stern warnings from Daniel. God was unwilling to let this Babylonian king claim all the praise for himself. God struck him down until such time as Nebuchadnezzar realized that Jehovah was sovereign Lord. In an earlier era, we see King David foolishly calling for a census of the army, contrary to the advice of his own commanders. There, too, God intervened and convicted David of his grievous sin (2 Sam. 24). In the case of Xerxes, God is still sovereign, but he does not warn or stop him from his display of self-glorification. The ruler of the universe allows this evil king to pursue his own fantasy. Xerxes is a pawn in the mind of the great chess master, but he does not know it.

Conspicuous consumption is a good description of this prolonged feasting in the palace at Susa. After celebrating for 180 days, it is time for a feast that will go on for another 7 days. The finest tapestries will be on display. The most expensive goblets will be on the tables. The best wine will be available, with no limits imposed by the king's staff. Drink as much as you like, as often as you want. Eat, drink, and be merry, for tomorrow we dine again. There is, seemingly, no limit to frivolity. Everyone is happy and full of wine. Even "the heart of the king was merry with wine" (1:10). In another part of the palace, "Queen Vashti also gave a feast for the women in the palace" (1:9). Persian custom, like that in Arabia today, stipulated that women and men celebrate separately, with wives guarded from the lecherous eyes of envious men. Even evildoers tend to set some parameters.

After seven days of drinking and carousing, the most powerful human on earth orders his seven "eunuchs" to "bring Queen Vashti before the king with her royal crown, in order to show the peoples and the princes her beauty, for she was lovely to look at" (1:11). The text here gives us some clues into the character of Persian society. There is obviously a harem of beautiful women being overseen by "eunuchs," castrated so as to deprive them of sexual desires. The harem is housed somewhere in or near the king's bedroom so that he can call upon them whenever he wished. Put into more contemporary language, these women are sex slaves, with one purpose in their lives. The one who most pleased the king is designated as queen. At present, that person is Vashti. She is stunningly beautiful. Xerxes wishes to put her on parade, not for her benefit, but for his. A trophy wife would further enhance his image as king. He follows protocol, commanding his staff of eunuchs to bring her in, wearing her crown.

There is one small problem. This woman refuses to appear. "At this the king became enraged and his anger burned within him" (1:12). The great despot, who promised to subjugate Greece and burn down Athens, cannot control his own wife. What irony! What monstrous embarrassment!

The text does not give us her rationale, but Josephus offers one possible explanation. According to him, some Chaldean sources asserted that Xerxes, in a drunken stupor, wanted her to be brought in naked, wearing only her crown.[6] Given what we know about Persian culture, and what we know about inhibitions during drunkenness, Josephus's explanation is probably valid. Drunken men, accustomed to sexual promiscuity, are known to engage in vile behavior. If in doubt, reflect on the dominant culture in Hollywood during their award ceremonies. Given Vashti's notorious beauty, "for she was lovely to look at," her refusal was probably justified. Her justification is not the point of the story, however, for a "savior" of God's people needs to enter center stage. But that will not occur until the seventh year of Xerxes' reign.

In the meantime, something must be done. If Vashti's refusal becomes known throughout the empire, no man will be able to control his own household. "There will be contempt and wrath in plenty" (1:18). The best lawyers in the land are called upon to draft legislation that will prevent such rebellion from becoming widespread. The law, never to be repealed, is both personal and universal. "Vashti is never again to come before King Ahasuerus," and "all women will give honor to their husbands, high and low alike" (1:19–20). Such legislation will become almost impossible to enforce, but it becomes the law of the Persian Empire. It puts the power of enforcement in the hands of husbands, who may be as cruel and immoral as the king issuing the decree. Spousal abuse lies in wait.

Discussion Starters

1. Is it permissible to use secular histories for purposes of understanding Scripture? Is it helpful? What is the major difference between Scripture and secular history? What do secular historians choose to ignore?

2. Why do Jewish scholars place such high value on the book of Esther? Why do Christian scholars often tend to deprecate the book of Esther?

3. Why do our Bibles call this king Ahasuerus, while secular historians refer to him as Xerxes?

4. Why does the writer of Esther ignore the military side of Persian history, when there is substantial information available which will shed light on the biblical account?

5. Why is it important that the king have "eunuchs" overseeing the harem?

6. Why is it important that the harem be populated with young virgins? What is that saying about the moral character of the Persian society?

7. What difficulties might one expect in the enforcement of this new decree, demanding honor from wives? Did Vashti's refusal constitute a violation of this law?

8. Does God's Word stipulate a proper relationship between wives and husbands (see Eph. 5:22–33)? Should wives be submissive to their husbands?

Notes

1. The Persian military, at this time, was estimated to number 100,000 to 150,000 combatants and 700 warships. For further details about the wars between Persia and Greece, see G. W. Botsford and C. A. Robinson Jr., *Greek History*, 4th ed. (New York: Macmillan, 1956), 112–46.

2. Richard Burke, *The Ancient World* (New York: McGraw-Hill, 1967), 128.

3. Ibid., 25.

4. Ibid.

5. John W. Lee, *The Persian Empire* (Chantilly, VA: The Great Courses, 2012), 92–93.

6. *The Life and Works of Flavius Josephus*, trans. William Whiston (New York: Holt, Rinehart and Winston, 1957), 334.

Chapter 2

A Jewish Orphan Becomes the New Queen

Scripture: Esther 2:1–18
Background reading: Genesis 38:1–30; Matthew 1:1–3

The Lapse of Time

As we begin to look at Esther 2, we quickly notice a lapse of time. The events recorded for us in this chapter do not follow immediately after those in Esther 1. We are reminded that royal decrees from King Xerxes went "throughout all his kingdom, for it is vast" (1:20). That obviously took a good deal of time and effort, giving the king opportunity to get over his intense anger. From secular sources we also know that it gave him time to wage an extensive military campaign against Greece. He had vowed earlier that he would burn down Athens and march across Europe. This, too, was a failure. His ego is badly bruised, so he "remembers Vashti and what she had done and what had been decreed against her" (2:1). In his mind, all his troubles could be attributed to her. None of this was his fault. A king without a queen! Plus a failed military expedition! What an anomaly!

We know from Esther 1 that Vashti had been deposed in the third year of his reign. We know, too, that Esther does not become queen until the seventh year of Xerxes' reign (2:16). That means that there are four years between those two events. What else is going on? What has transpired during those intervening years?

The Search for a Replacement

It is the "young men who attended him" who offer a solution. These young men are eunuchs, just as was the case in King Nebuchadnezzar's court. They suggest that searches be made throughout the empire for the most beautiful young virgins that could be found. They suggest that every province, from India to Greece to Egypt, be searched. "Let beautiful young virgins be sought out for the king . . . and gather all the beautiful young virgins to the harem in Susa" (2:2–3). Physical appearance was paramount. Virgin status was demanded and emphasized. With 127 provinces in the empire, this probably resulted in three hundred to four hundred young women being rounded up and taken captive. By camel, by horse, by donkey, or by foot they were taken to the capital. They were guarded by eunuchs so that their virginity would not be compromised. The king was fussy!

When Boko Haran does this in northern Nigeria, we recognize it as slave trade for sexual gratification. When ISIS does this in Afghanistan or Syria, we again howl in protest. This is evil! Incredibly evil! The same standard should apply to Persia and King Ahasuerus. The label of "oriental despot" is then well deserved. This is not a simple beauty contest to see who gets top billing. This is kidnapping on a massive scale. The parents of these young ladies, with a few possible exceptions, are not going to send their daughters to Susa with their blessing. They know how their daughters are going to be exploited, for they know why harems exist. Even King David and King Solomon were guilty of such behavior. This clearly flies in the face of all God's commands. We cannot justify this.

The Appearance of Mordecai

Before we meet the next queen of Persia, we need to become acquainted with Mordecai. The first bit of information about him is that he is a Jew. He is living in the citadel of Susa and is one of those brought into Babylon as a captive from Jerusalem. If he were old enough, he probably could have gone back to Jerusalem with Zerubbabel and Jeshua in 538 BC, when Cyrus issued his edict, but he, like so many others, chose to stay living in Persia. The year is probably 480 or 479 BC, sixty years since Persia had conquered Babylon. We don't know Mordecai's age, but we know his lineage. He is a Benjamite and a descendant of Kish, the father of King Saul (1 Sam. 9:1–3). As the story unfolds, that will become part and parcel of his conflict with Haman, who is a descendant of Agag, the king of the Amalekites (Exod. 17:8–16; 1 Sam. 15:1–10). More of that later, but we also need to note his name, a variation of the Babylonian god Marduk. The same was true for Daniel and his three friends, who were given names after the idols of Babylon (Dan. 1:6–7). He probably had a Hebrew name, too, but that is not important to the story line. He is a government official with a pagan name living in a corrupt, immoral culture. He works close to the house for the harem, so he can keep contact with his adopted daughter.

Mordecai had obviously done much to guard and guide this beautiful young lady, but only one thing is specifically mentioned: Do not tell anyone that you are a Jew. The text is explicit about his Jewish lineage but is equally specific about her not divulging her ancestry. Why? What dangers could be associated with that? As we read through the book of Ezra, we know that King Cyrus had bestowed unusual privileges, licenses, and wealth on those who chose to return to Jerusalem (Ezra 1:4–11; 6:4–12). We know, too, that there were numerous enemies of those returning Jews and that King Cambyses had used the military to stop the rebuilding of the temple. Persia was then and still is a pagan empire, with a wide variety of idols being worshipped. Yes, there were unusual demonstrations of God's favor on his people, as demonstrated by Cyrus and Darius, but those were the exceptions and not the rule. The Persian populace, for the most part, are enemies of God and hate his laws and the people who worship him. The great conflict between the people of God and the followers of Satan is always there, sometimes just under the surface, sometimes open and flagrant.

Esther Pleases the King

Through Mordecai we become acquainted with Hadassah, better known as Esther. Her parents are both dead, but her cousin has taken her in as his own daughter. Her name is a Persian variation of Ishtar, a Babylonian goddess. The most obvious quality that she possessed was "a beautiful figure" that was lovely to look at. Lecherous eyes longed to see her. Among the hundreds of young virgins in the harem, she stood out and got the attention of the master eunuch, Hegai, "who had charge of the women." Esther "pleased him and won his favor" (2:9). In contrast with the regimen imposed on Daniel and his three friends, who had to endure three years of preparation (Dan. 1:5), these young women had to submit to a beautifying process, "six months with oil of myrrh and six months with spices and ointments" (2:12). External beauty was priceless and paramount. Obedience was demanded, while wisdom was ignored.

In contrast with Daniel and his three friends, there is no indication that Esther or Mordecai objected to this process of cultural cultivation. There are no recorded protests or requests for exemption. As we read on, there is extensive description of the facilities for the king's harem and the expectations of its members. If they please the king, they might get to sleep another night in his bed. If not, they are shunted off to less desirable quarters and are labeled as concubines. Concubines may never marry and will never become mothers. They are doomed to live as slaves to a vile master. On the basis of the text, both Mordecai and Esther appear to be compromised persons. Either they did not know the law of God, or they chose to ignore it. Either way, they are guilty. Sleeping with a pagan king outside the bonds of marriage is and was adultery. Becoming a willing accomplice in sex trafficking is evil. No prophets are sent to warn them or call them to repentance.

Where Is God?

As we reflect on the book of Daniel, we notice some significant differences. From the opening pages of Daniel, we see the hand of our sovereign God at work. God puts dreams into King Nebuchadnezzar's head. God endows Daniel and his friends with uncanny wisdom. God presents his Son, Jesus Christ, as "the stone cut out of the mountain, not by human hands" (Dan. 2:34). God allows the three friends to be thrown into the fiery furnace so that King Nebuchadnezzar can see the Savior of his people at work. God punishes Nebuchadnezzar with insanity for the sin of pride. God is everywhere. In Esther, the opposite appears to be true. God is nowhere on the pages of this book, yet we ought to remember that he is sovereign everywhere all the time. He controls events and persons by his sovereign will, but he also allows people and nations to exercise their evil inclinations.

When we reflect on the background readings from Genesis 38, we see Judah, one of the twelve sons of Jacob, engage in perpetually evil behavior. He is co-habiting with a Canaanite woman and producing multiple children by her. He leaves home and solicits sex with a street prostitute, who happens to be his daughter-in-law. Tamar becomes pregnant by him and produces twin boys. How evil can you get? Yet three of those persons appear in the genealogy of Jesus Christ (Matt. 1:3). God allowed that behavior and had it recorded on the pages of Scripture, not to demonstrate his wrath against sin, but his mercy and his grace toward his chosen ones. God is doing something similar with Esther and Mordecai because the enemies of God want to exterminate the entire nation of Israel. We need to keep perspective if we are to understand the book and actions of Esther. God is going to allow Esther to please this immoral monarch in such a way that he chooses her from all the virgins to be the next queen of Persia. As Mordecai will later suggest, she was chosen for such a time as this (4:15). As a servant of the one who rules the nations with a double-edged sword, she will be the instrument used to save his people from genocide.

Where Are Ezra and Nehemiah?

Other enigmas that beg for resolution are questions about the silence of Ezra and Nehemiah. Both of these godly men live in Persia soon after Esther serves as queen and Mordecai serves as prime minister. Both of them must have celebrated the Feast of Purim on numerous occasions. Ezra appears on the pages of Scripture during the seventh year of King Artaxerxes, which translates as the year 458 BC, twenty-one years after Esther becomes queen. Ezra is a gifted scribe or writer, who is also the most qualified theologian, but he never mentions Esther or Mordecai or the Feast of Purim. Ezra writes extensively about the building of the temple and events surrounding it but never credits these two agents of God who are responsible for preventing the extermination of the Jewish people. Ezra is also God's agent to teach the remnant in Jerusalem and Judah the elements of proper worship. That omission becomes even more puzzling if Ezra was the writer of the book of Esther, as Augustine and others surmise.

This mystery becomes even more pronounced when we realize that there is a gap of sixty years between the events that Ezra describes in chapter 6 and chapter 7 of his book. Those are the very years where Esther was queen and Mordecai "was second in rank to King Ahasuerus" (Esther 10:3). He must have known about them, yet he chose not to write about them. That mystery can be explained only by the reminder that "all Scripture is breathed by God," as the apostle Paul reminded Timothy.

We note a similar pattern with Nehemiah, the cupbearer to King Artaxerxes. Even though he recalls many of Israel's flagrant sins, he, too, ignores the situation in the citadel of Persia. He, like Ezra, focuses almost exclusively on the spiritual needs and challenges in Jerusalem. Both of these theological giants concentrate their writings on the restoration of God-ordained worship in the Promised Land. The pattern reminds us of the contrast between Revelation 3 and Revelation 4. That third chapter is focused on the earthly situation in the seven churches, full of sin and shortcomings. Chapter 4, by contrast, elevates us into the throne room of heaven, where God is praised and worshipped. Ezra and Nehemiah are God's appointed agents of restoration and renewal.

Esther is a somewhat pathetic person needing reformation. All are part of divine revelation.

Discussion Starters

1. What characteristics do you associate with King Ahasuerus? Is he a good king?

2. What motivates the young men to orchestrate an empire-wide search for beautiful young virgins?

3. Would parents welcome the king's agents who come looking for a potential queen? Would some parents relish that role for their daughters?

4. Why is it important that Mordecai be identified as a descendant of King Saul? Does that designation confer status for him? Or, does that denigrate him?

5. Should Esther have devised some plan to avoid becoming the queen? How might she have done that?

6. How is the sovereignty of God being demonstrated in this chapter? In this book?

7. Is it justified for both Ezra and Nehemiah to ignore the historical record of Esther and Mordecai? Was the Feast of Purim important to them? Was that feast important to God?

Chapter 3

The Seeds of Warfare Are Being Sown

Scripture: Esther 2:19–3:15
Background reading: Exodus 17:8–16; Deuteronomy 25:17–19; 1 Samuel 15:1–9, 32–33

As we continue our reading in the book of Esther, we might conclude that the events presented are nice, neat demonstrations of coincidence. It just so happens, by chance, that Mordecai happened to be in the right place at the right time to hear about this conspiracy against King Ahasuerus. That would be the secular reaction to this event. But we, as students of God's Word, reflecting on the messages from Daniel, know that providence must replace coincidence. The sovereign Ruler of nations is controlling and allowing this event, too. He permits it and knows the future. He will direct it for his own glory. Two men conspire to kill the king. Mordecai overhears the plot. For Mordecai, this was an occasion to prove his allegiance to the emperor. For the emperor, it was a fortunate report that spared his life. For Esther, it was probably welcome news that her husband of five years would live for another day. Esther has been queen now for five years (3:7) and probably has become immune to the daily doses of palace politics. Quite naturally, she forwards her uncle's message to the king. The rumor is validated, the villains are hanged on the gallows, and life goes on. The incident is recorded in the public record, but no rewards are doled out.

We are informed of a second event, but no rationale is offered for it. Ahasuerus, for no apparent reason, elevates Haman to the second highest office in the empire. This is no simple appointment but a significant event affecting the course of Jewish history. Matthew Henry reminds us,

> The king took a fancy to him (princes are not bound to give reasons for their favours), made him his favourite, his confidant, his prime minister of state. Such a commanding influence the court then had that (contrary to the proverb) those whom it blessed the country blessed too; for all men adored this rising sun, and the king's servants were particularly commanded to bow before him and to do him reverence (Es 3:2), and they did so. I wonder what the king saw in Haman that was commendable or meritorious; it is plain that he was not a man of honour or justice, of any true courage or steady conduct, but proud, and passionate, and revengeful; yet was he promoted, and caressed, and there was none so great as he. Princes' darlings are not always worthies.

Haman is given all the trappings of highest royalty and allowed his own throne. When he speaks, he speaks for the king. He expects every person to bow before him, treating him as lord of the manor. The fact that such allegiance was commanded by the king (3:2) tells us something about the king. This king is easily duped. Whether it is blind allegiance to a special friend or greedy desire for the stupendous bribe being offered, he becomes the enemy of God's people and the enemy of God. His consent to Haman's horrendous demand confers guilt upon the king, equal to that on his prime minister. Ahasuerus's behavior reminds us of similar actions by King Darius I, as recorded for us in Daniel 6. Shortly after the Medes and the Persians had jointly conquered Babylon, some enemies of Daniel persuade King Darius to proclaim a rule that all persons must worship him alone and give allegiance to no other. Darius foolishly buys into their scheme and inadvertently condemns Daniel to death. God allowed that, too, but turned it to great advantage by shutting the lions' mouths. Consequently, the king issued a decree that "in all my dominion people are to tremble and fear before the God of Daniel" (Dan. 6:26). Oftentimes we do not know how sovereignty works, but we relish the outcome. The Jews loved this new edict, but idolaters loathed it. It is the height of irony that Jewish scholars today despise the book of Daniel but love the book of Esther.

Mordecai refuses to bow down. For him, that would be an act of worship. Co-workers and friends persist in reminding him of his duty, but he continues to defy the king's orders. He has earlier demonstrated his allegiance to the empire, but he will not condescend to worship. The text does not reference the first or second commandments but gives us bold, dangerous, and repeated actions. To defy the king of Persia is to sign a death warrant. In that respect, Mordecai begins to look like the Daniel of old. He is willing to die before he complies with an evil edict.

Upon reflection, the plot thickens. Haman is furious, much like Ahasuerus was when Vashti refused to come at his beck and call. His reaction, like that of the king earlier, is going to shift the course of the empire. Haman is not just a lone, offended individual. He is one remaining vestige of a tribe condemned to extermination by the Lord of heaven and earth. Haman is an Agagite, a descendant of King Agag, the ruler of the Amalekites. God had instructed Moses and Joshua to destroy the entire nation of the Amalekites because of their opposition to the Israelites as they wandered in the wilderness. The Lord had been explicit: "I will utterly blot out the memory of Amalek from under heaven" (Exod. 17:14). The righteous Judge of heaven and earth would not tolerate opposition of that sort. He emphasized that later when he told Moses: "Remember what Amalek did to you on the way as you came out of Egypt." "You shall blot out the memory of Amalek from under heaven" (Deut. 25:17, 29). God is a righteous Judge whose self-described name is Jealous!

Delayed Justice

Much later, when Saul becomes the first earthly king of Israel, God instructs him to kill Agag, the king of the Amalekites. As we read through 1 Samuel 15, we are struck by the explicit commands coming directly from God through his prophet Samuel: "Thus says the Lord of hosts, I have noted what Amalek did to Israel in opposing them on the way when they came up out of Egypt. Now go and strike Amalek and devote to destruction all that they have. Do not spare them, but kill both man and woman, child and infant, ox and sheep, camel and donkey" (1 Sam. 15:1–3). Our Western mindsets, heavily influenced by democratic philosophy, find such commands very difficult to accept. We might concede the guilt of the king in that instance, but we would want to excuse the women, the children, the animals, and the entire nation. But the command comes from God. The Amalekites wanted to destroy the nation of Israel. But Israel is God's chosen people. Therefore God is jealous. In his wrath, he orders the destruction of the entire enemy nation of King Agag. We need to be reminded of this important truth as we later read about the Persians' desire to kill all of the Jews in the empire. It will also help us understand and accept the Jewish slaughter of their enemies.

Saul's army begins to destroy that nation, but Saul foolishly chooses to spare Agag and disobeys God's explicit command. For that disobedience, Saul pays a heavy price. At that point, Samuel, the prophet of God, becomes the executioner for God. He draw his own sword "and hacked Agag to pieces before the Lord in Gilgal" (1 Sam. 15:32–33). The wrath of God against disobedience is then graphically portrayed once again. We do well to learn from this biblical account and recognize that most of the Persian nation resembles Agag. God, the ultimate author of this book, introduces us to Haman as a role model, driven by pride and self-centered worship. The antagonist is Haman, representing Agag. The protagonist is Mordecai, representing King Saul. The seeds of war are sown.

Ten Thousand Talents of Silver?

The seeds of warfare are watered when Haman discovers that Mordecai is a Jew. His hatred is intensified. Now, he must not only kill Mordecai. He must also kill every Jew in the empire. He probably recognizes that Queen Esther is also a Jew. He is committed to genocide. Like Hitler in our day, he is devoted to their extermination. Such a campaign takes time, not only to plan but also to execute. Scheduling a date for such an empire-wide campaign is important. Trusting to a roll of the Pur (dice or lots), they roll them day after day and month after month until the Pur settles on "the twelfth month, which is the month of Adar" (3:7). Again, there is no accident or happenstance. God, the sovereign, controls even this. With the timing settled, the enemy of God's people makes his move. He needs the approval of his friend, the king. In his attempts to persuade the king, Haman admits that "their laws are different from those of every other people" (3:8). Without realizing it, Haman is acknowledging their special character and the uniqueness of the laws by which they live. To cement the deal, he offers the king a bribe: ten thousand talents of silver. If the king had any accounting sense, he would have laughed in scorn. That enormous amount would be approximately equal to two-thirds of the annual revenue for the entire empire. Where would Haman ever acquire such wealth? The king asks no questions but further implicates himself in this evil scheme. Is he duped again, or is he co-conspirator?

Very probably Ahasuerus knew exactly where such wealth could be found. The edict that he signed included the plundering of all Jewish property. That included the temple in Jerusalem, with all its gold and silver. That included the property of every Jewish family in the entire empire. Much of that wealth had originally been the property of Persia, but King Cyrus had given it to the Jews who were returning to Jerusalem (Ezra 1:8–10). Haman must have chafed at the thought of paying taxes to support the worship of this Jewish God. These evil characters knew about Cambyses's attempt to stop the rebuilding of the temple in 530 BC, but they also knew about Darius I's finding Cyrus's edict which allowed the Jews to tax the provinces and accumulate whatever they needed (Ezra 6:6–12).

Official proclamations fan out over the empire, to all 127 provinces. Every Jew must be destroyed, killed, and annihilated, young and old, men, women, and children. And their property is to be plundered. Take whatever you can grab! The edict was announced in every language, in every script, in every city and town, probably "on swift horses." The date is set and publicly proclaimed: "on the thirteenth day of the twelfth month" every citizen is given the right and the duty to murder every Jew that they can find and "plunder their goods." Nothing secretive! No stealth! Just wholesale slaughter. The chapter ends on a sordid note: "the king and Haman sat down to drink, but the city of Susa was thrown into confusion" (3:15).

The decree of guilt is not confined to Haman, wicked and evil though he be. King Ahasuerus and the Persian nation have cast themselves as enemies of God's people. Thereby, they have become the enemies of God. They will pay a price. Rest assured.

Discussion Starters

1. The discovery of the assassination plot against the king appears to be mere happenstance. How do we come to recognize it as providence?

2. Who is the author of Esther? Is he formulating a master plot that will culminate in his advantage? Does the book of Esther begin to read like a suspense novel? What qualities demonstrate that?

3. How does the repeated description of Haman the Agagite portray him as an evil person, an enemy of God's people?

4. Is it probable that both Haman and Ahasuerus knew about Cyrus's generosity to the returning Jews? How would they have known? Would they be inclined to approve such generosity?

5. In trying to understand the political climate in Persia, would Haman have been a follower of Cambyses or of Darius? Would he have given support to the Samaritans' efforts?

6. Ezra tells us much about the positive treatment of the Jews by Cyrus and Darrius but does not mention the Persian attempts to kill them and take their property. Why this significant omission?

7. What advantages are gained by having the correct chronological sequence of events? Does that chronology help us understand the nature and background of this war between Persia and the Jews? Does knowing that Esther occurred before Ezra help us gain a correct perspective?

8. Does the fact that Ahasuerus asks no questions about the ten thousand talents of silver implicate him as a co-conspirator?

Chapter 4

Confusion, Crying, and Chaos

Scripture: Esther 4
Background reading: Matthew 16:21–23; 17:22–23; 20:17–19

The opening line of Esther 4 is revealing. It is the key to understanding this chapter. The text tells us that "Mordecai learned all that had been done." Mordecai is apparently an official in the Persian government. He has insider information. He knows exactly how much money Haman had offered in his bribe to the king (4:7). He knows that his co-workers had informed Haman about the fact that he, Mordecai, is a Jew and would not bow down to him. He knows that his co-workers want to use him as a test case, wanting to know whether a Jew could refuse to bow down and get by with such behavior (3:4). He knows, too, that his refusal had made Haman furious. He probably surmised that his personal actions had initiated the decree to slaughter all the Jews in the empire. His behavior was going to cause the death of millions of Jewish people.[1] He also knew that Haman was an incredibly evil person, willing to use a single personal offense as a pretext to annihilate hundreds of thousands of innocent women and children. Haman's depth of wickedness knows no bounds. The king is complicit in his evil plan.

Mordecai is not confused, but everyone else probably was. Decrees had been issued in every province, in every language, in every script. There were pamphlets posted in Jerusalem in the Hebrew language. Everybody on the street could read them. Millions of Jews must have been wondering: What have we done to deserve this? Why is King Ahasuerus issuing an order to have us all killed? Why are the people around us, our neighbors, given the right to come into our villages, our homes, our cities, with a license to kill us? Why are they being encouraged "to plunder our goods"? Have we done something to bring this about? What crimes have we committed? Why are so many of our neighbors consenting to such genocide? Why did they choose the "thirteenth day of the twelfth month" (3:13)? What is so special about that date? Also, this edict was issued on the thirteenth day of the first month (3:12). That gives us essentially a full year before this will happen. Why announce it so early? What is significant about the thirteenth day?

Mordecai's reaction is fully expected. He is stunned. He is distraught. He takes off his clothes, puts on sackcloth and ashes, walks into the central square of Susa, and starts screaming. He "cried out with a loud and bitter cry." He is not ashamed, but he is terribly torn. He caused this. What must he do? He heads for the palace gate. He knows that even though he is a government official, he cannot enter. Going through the gate dressed in sackcloth is a ticket to death. Only nice clothes are permitted within the palace walls. If he so much as passes through the gate, the guards will kill him. If someone dressed appropriately approaches the king without being called, that person will, ordinarily, also die. This king has no mercy.

The reaction among the Jewish population, scattered across the empire, is similar to that of Mordecai. They, too, lay in sackcloth and ashes. There was great "mourning, with fasting and weeping and lamenting" (4:3). The Jews were a minority within the empire. There was no prospect of defeating the government forces or winning such a war. To understand their predicament, it would be helpful to reflect on the genocide that occurred in the African nation of Rwanda in 1994. Ever since this little country had gained its independence from Belgium in 1962, there had been ethnic tension. The Hutu tribe, comprising 85 percent of the population, had gained control of the government. The Tutsi tribe represented only 15 percent of the population and was excluded from the halls of power. In 1994 the Hutu government officials, without justification, encouraged ordinary citizens to take up arms against the Tutsi people, kill them, and plunder their goods. Before peace was restored, eight hundred thousand Tutsis lay dead in the streets and another three million had fled the country.

That is the type of situation the Jews faced in Persia at this point in their history. Political tensions had been boiling just beneath the surface, with Cambyses sending the Persian army to stop the rebuilding of the temple in 530 BC. Before that, the citizens of Samaria tried to take over the worship of Jehovah in Jerusalem (see Ezra 4). Now, for reasons not understood by the masses, there is an edict issued for the slaughter of all the Jews in the empire. Naturally, they weep and mourn and lament.

One of the mystifying aspects of this book is that there is no call for repentance and no message from God. There is no confession of sin, even though it appears that the Jewish population had become acculturated within this pagan society. Seemingly, there is no prophet of God assigned to this place or time with clarion calls for repentance. This lack of spiritual fervor may help to explain why the books of Ezra and Nehemiah make no mention of Esther or the Feast of Purim, even though they follow soon after. One possible explanation might lie in the book of Joel, which does call for repentance and describes some situations comparable to that during the time of Esther. But no definitive date for Joel has been established, so this explanation remains as mere conjecture.

Queen Esther is confused. She has been sheltered and protected and ignored within the palace walls. She is the queen of Persia, but in name only. Her husband has not confided in her. The eunuchs in charge of the harem are not informing her. Her husband has not invited her to his bed for a month. Her closest confidant is acting very strangely. Why is her cousin ranting and railing in sackcloth and ashes in front of the palace gate? Does he not know the consequences? I better bring him some appropriate clothes, something regal and soft and appealing. She sends him some clothes, but he refuses to take them. Why?

Esther needs to know what is happening. She sends one of her loyal servants, Hatach, to inquire. Mordecai holds nothing back. He tells Hatach "all that had happened to him" (4:6). He provides a full dossier for his cousin, including the full amount of the bribe that Haman had offered her husband. He sends a copy of the written decree, signed by her husband, the king. She had to experience a deep sense of betrayal, knowing that her husband of five years was willing to have her killed in exchange for wealth. She must have wondered: Does he love me at all? Why has he not called for me these many weeks?

Role Reversals

About this point in the story, an interesting development occurs. Prior to this point, Mordecai issues all the commands. He is the one who "commanded her not to make it known" that she was a Jew (2:10). Later on, we are told that "Esther had obeyed Mordecai just as when she was brought up by him" (2:20). Mordecai continues in that role and now "commands her to go to the king to beg his favor and plead with him on behalf of her people" (4:8). The order itself is a reversal: Do not hide your identity any longer. Acknowledge your lineage. Admit that you are a Jew, scheduled to die. Esther is a stunningly beautiful queen of Persia, but she is also an obedient orphan girl. She does whatever her cousin tells her to do, until she reads the edict and learns about her impending death. Esther suddenly reverses roles. She becomes the queen, worthy of the title. She knows the laws of the land. She sends a message to Mordecai, informing him of standard operating procedure in Persia. The king has the power of the sword. If he does not want to see you or hear from you, he can have you put to death on the spot, no trial and no judge.

In one sense, Esther is offering an excuse. She does not want to risk her life. She does not want to tempt the king, who has been ignoring her and finding satisfaction with others. She reminds us of Moses, who pleaded with God to recuse him from confronting Pharaoh (Exod. 3:10–19). Moses knew that Pharaoh had put a price on his head and wanted to kill him (Exod. 2:15). But Moses eventually went, not once but multiple times. Esther's reluctance also reflects the initial reaction of Isaiah, who is confronted, not by King Ahasuerus, but by the King of heaven. In contrast to the power of God, Isaiah pleads, "Woe is me! For I am lost; for I am a man of unclean lips" (Isa. 6:5). Isaiah capitulates, too, knowingly risking his life as he confronts the evil kings of Israel and Judah.

God did not accept the excuses of either Moses or Isaiah. Mordecai does not accept the excuse of Esther. He offers her one of the most powerful arguments found in the entire book: "Do not think... you will escape any more than all the other Jews" (4:13). If you go to the king, you might die. But if you do not go to the king, you will surely die. He follows that with a statement asserting the sovereignty of God. If you refuse, "relief and deliverance will rise for the Jews from another place" (4:14). He might have been reflecting on the writings of Jeremiah. He might have recalled messages from the book of Daniel. The implication is clear: God will preserve a remnant of his special people. God will not allow the Jewish people to disappear from the earth. Mordecai continues with a dynamic challenge: "Who knows whether you have not come to the kingdom for such a time as this?" (4:14). My dear sweet orphan girl, you might have been chosen because of your beauty, but there may be a greater purpose behind it all.

Esther's response is most appropriate. She commands her cousin, "Go, gather all the Jews to be found in Susa, and hold a fast on my behalf, and do not eat or drink for three days, night or day" (4:16). The text does not mention prayer, but that is historically associated with fasting. Esther has confessed that she is a Jew, one of those despised by the masses and scheduled to die, but she also acknowledges the power of God. She specifically demands a fast for "three days," not unlike the three days from Good Friday to Easter. In one real sense, Esther is a foreshadowing of Jesus Christ.[2] She is willing to die so that she might save her people. She is not the sinless, perfect Lamb of God, but she is one who carries the sins of her people. She is willing to die, just as her Savior willingly and repeatedly told his followers why he had to go to Jerusalem. Her commitment is adequate reason to give Jewish scholars an excuse to treat her as a heroine of the faith

Discussion Starters

1. Why did Mordecai command Esther not to reveal that she was a Jew? Why does the text inform us that Mordecai was a Jew (2:5)? What does that tell us about Jewish acceptance within the empire?

2. What evidence do we have for concluding that Mordecai was a government official?

3. How might Mordecai have learned the amount of the bribery offered by Haman?

4. How might the Jewish population have reacted to the publication of the edicts against them? Could they have fled the empire and gone elsewhere?

5. What possible plans might the Jews have devised once they realized that there was a time lag of one year before their scheduled execution?

6. What might the Jews have decided concerning their possessions, their houses, their animals, their jewelry, knowing that the Persians would plunder them?

7. How would one account for the role reversal between Esther and Mordecai? What precipitated it?

8. Is it consistent with Scripture to think of Esther as a foreshadowing of Christ? Are there other women in the Bible who might also earn that distinction? Sarah? Miriam? Ruth?

Notes

1. The number of Jewish people in the empire can only be estimated. We know that fifty thousand had gone to Jerusalem when Cyrus issued his decree in 538 BC. We know, too, large numbers chose to remain in Persia at that time. We also know that large numbers had fled to Egypt when Nebuchadnezzar had attacked Jerusalem. We know, too, that David had conducted a census and had counted "800,000 valiant men who had drawn the sword" (2 Sam. 24:9).
2. I hesitate to refer to her as a type of Christ, but see some obvious similarities that would qualify as foreshadowing.

Chapter 5

From Feasting to Fasting to Feasting

Scripture: Esther 5
Background reading: Daniel 10:1–9; Ezra 8:21–32

Whenever we attempt to understand historical events, timing of those events is often important. Queen Esther had commanded Mordecai to gather all the Jews in the capital city of Susa and to hold a fast on her behalf for three days. Traditionally, a fast would last for just one day. But the situation is now desperate. All of God's people are threatened with death. Edicts are posted in every province and every city. The date for execution is duly noted. The populace responds to Mordecai's call to action. Dressed in sackcloth and covered with ashes (4:3), the Jewish residents in the city fasted and prayed for three days straight. Although the text does not mention prayer, that was always associated with fasting. Very probably, this massive effort was noticed by neighbors and government officials. Knowing that the Jews were hated by large segments of the population, it might seem surprising to find no overt resistance to it. The text is silent.

To find clarity, we need to look both backward and forward. Looking backward into a slightly earlier time, we find Daniel fasting and praying, not for three days but for three weeks (Dan. 10:2). At the end of that period he receives a vision of a "man clothed in linen" (Dan 10:5) who is clearly the pre-incarnate Christ. His characteristics match those given to us in Ezekiel 1:26–28 and in Revelation 1:13–17. Daniel had earlier seen images of Christ in the fiery furnace, saving his three friends from incineration. These are obviously reminders to Daniel about the sovereignty of God and the way in which "the stone cut out of the mountain" (Dan. 2:34) would break in pieces the empires that were to follow. Daniel saw that happen during his lifetime when the Medes and Persians descended on Babylon. That message must have become part of Jewish tradition and lore and instruction. Esther and Mordecai should have been familiar with it. That may have intensified their prayers.

We also have the advantage of looking ahead and knowing the book of Ezra. It articulates marvelous ways by which God protected his people. The account of Ezra spending three days of fasting and praying at the river Ahava ought to fascinate us. He had been informing the king that Jehovah would watch over and protect them on their four-month journey to Jerusalem, even though they were carrying vast amounts of gold and silver through crime-infested areas. With no military protection visible, every penny of that wealth was delivered to the Holy City. The invisible hand of the Lord was protecting them all the way. The Lord of hosts was watching over them. The sovereign God was restraining all the highway robbers along their route.

To understand this phase of Esther, we need to transfer that sovereign hand of God to the city of Susa.[1] There is the overarching theme of feasting, fasting, and feasting, given to us as a framework for story development. Underneath, however, is the hand of God at work. With the appointment of Esther to the queen's position, we see another instance where "the Most High rules the kingdom of men and gives it to whom he will" (Dan. 4:17, 25, 32). Esther is not chosen queen because of her physical beauty, but because God wanted her there. Just as God planted dreams in Nebuchadnezzar's head (Dan. 2:28), so the Father in heaven put Esther in the palace and gave her both courage and wisdom. She does not know if she will live or die when she enters the throne room, but she employs a strategy that will eventually prevent the destruction of her people. That is God at work.

The book of Esther reads like a well-crafted novel. There is progressive character development, giving us personality glimpses into the lives of Esther, of Ahasuerus, of Mordecai, and of Haman. Esther is no longer a virgin waiting to be seduced but a regal commander, relying on prayer, now dressed in elegant robes. Mordecai is no longer a despondent, screaming victim of anti-Semitism but a confident, strategizing leader who knows that God will provide help from some quarter, if not from Esther. The king is sympathetic to the wife he has been ignoring, while fawning over his close friend and delighted that he has been invited to the queen's table. Haman, meanwhile, is the personification of narcissism and evil. He gloats on his being invited, and, apparently, is ignorant of the queen's ethnic roots. He is full of conflicting emotions, rejoicing at his exalted position in the empire but full of hatred against the Jew who refuses to bow before him. As Haman gathers an audience to hear his boasts and great accomplishments, he seeks the advice of his equally evil wife, Zeresh. It is his wife, mentioned by name four times, who offers the quickest solution to his quandary. Build a gallows high enough for all to observe and then hang that offensive Jew on it. Let the whole city see who is master and who deserves to die.

Contrasts and Comparisons

One of the dominant themes in the book of Esther is the contrast between feasting and fasting. Esther 1 begins with a feast that lasted for 180 days, only to be followed with another feast that lasted a mere seven days. The king has his ostentatious display, but so does Queen Vashti. Palace décor, table decorations, and wall hangings are highlighted, all to show the splendor and glory of this evil, pagan empire. The menu, however, is ignored, with one exception. We do not know what they ate, but we do know what they drank. Wine was in abundance with everyone encouraged to drink as much as they wished. Varying degrees of inebriation are assumed, further casting a pall over the enemies of God's people. This vainglorious display of earthly riches results in the deposition of the queen and wholesale kidnapping of young women in every province of the kingdom. Marriage is supposed to follow biblical norms, but not under this administration. Find the most glamorous virgins in the empire, beautify them as much as humanly possible, and put them in my harem.

By contrast, the Jews find it necessary to forego food and beverages as an expression of complete dependence on God. Their symbolic leader, the uncle of young Esther, demonstrates in the city square by loud and bitter cries, setting a very public contrast to all the festivities of the Persians. He remonstrates, not in the confines of his home, but in the heart of the city, at the king's gate. The gate serves as a wall of separation. There is the implied contrast between Jews and Persians, which will subtly meld into the contrast between good and evil. Esther, meanwhile, is historically compromised by her participation in the harem but emerges as a master politician who is coyly planning the entrapment of her archenemy, Haman.

Esther enters the king's courtyard dressed in royal robes, designed to arouse the appetite of her husband, who is enamored with finery and regal splendors. He notices and bids her welcome. She does not make her plea or state her case. She is too clever for that. She invites him to a feast that she herself has prepared. She knows his love for feasts. He is known as the master feast planner. She knows his appetite for ostentatious display. When asked what her wish and request might be, she delays and invites him to a second feast. She insists that evil Haman be invited too.

Haman Is Incited to Violence

What happens next appears to be mere happenstance. Haman, brimming with pride and self-aggrandizement, has to pass through the city gate on the way to his luxurious home. There sits that despicable Jew. He won't rise. He won't bow. He won't tremble. Haman's blood comes close to the boiling point. What is he to do? How can he make this man realize how important he is? The insolence of that man almost drives him mad. But pride dominates. Does anyone know who alone has been invited to the queen's banquet? Does my family know why I came home late this evening? I have to tell them.

Zeresh and the neighbors have to hear what I have to tell them. As I climb to the pinnacle of self-glorification, I should also tell them about my bank accounts, my promotions within the government, and my extended family. Do you know how many children I have fathered? Do you know my rank in the Persian hierarchy? Do you know that I am going to another state banquet tomorrow? Do you know that Queen Esther has invited no one except the king and me?

Life would be splendid, glorious, except for one thing! I have to pass through the city gate again and be ignored by that despicable Jew. That is worse than rain on a parade. He probably will sit there and pretend as though he did not even see me. What audacity!

His wife, Zeresh, and all his friends offer a simple solution: Have him killed. You can do it. The king will continue to grant you your every wish. Ask him first thing in the morning. In the meanwhile, build a gallows on which to hang him. Make it high, seventy-five feet or so. The Jews will all see it and know that you must honor this noble Haman. He deserves it.

Irony is about to explode in our ears. Human authority seemingly takes center stage, but divine sovereignty is about to rule the roost. God will soon demonstrate that he is the great choreographer!

Discussion Starters

1. As you read through the background passage from Daniel 10, did you realize that "the man in linen" was the pre-incarnate Jesus Christ? Did you catch the similarities with the passages from Ezekiel 1 and Revelation 1? How does that help our comprehension of Esther 5?

2. As you read through the passage from Ezra 8, did you catch the irony of Ezra's refusal to ask for military escort from King Artaxerxes? What does that say about Ezra's faith? What does it say about the faith of the thousands of persons who went with him?

3. Was Esther deliberate and conniving in her plan of addressing the king? Or, was she operating as a pawn in the hand of God? Did God give her a clear plan of action to follow?

4. The text emphasizes the word "feast" six times in this chapter. Does that give us a clue as to how we should interpret these events?

5. Mordecai realizes that his refusal to honor Haman is what precipitated the edict to kill and plunder all the Jews in the empire. Could he have changed the course of history if he had stood and bowed whenever Haman came by? Should he have done such?

6. The text tells us that Haman "was filled with wrath" when Mordecai refused to honor him. What does that tell us about the character of Haman? How is his character further eroded?

7. Zeresh is mentioned by name and is given credit for offering her husband a solution. Does that make her an accomplice, worthy of death?

8. What clues can we find in the text to convince us that God is controlling all the events in this potential disaster?

Notes

1. One of the more helpful commentaries on Esther is that by Joyce G. Baldwin, *Esther: An Introduction and Commentary* (Downers Grove, IL: InterVarsity Press, 1984). She frequently appeals to the sovereignty of God as the best explanation for various events.

Chapter 6

The Turning of the Tide

Scripture: Esther 6–7:6

The Persian palace at Susa is quiet. Queen Esther had graciously hosted a feast for the two most important men in the empire. Attendance was tightly controlled. No great issues had been explored, but wine was in abundance. Tomorrow is another day. Tomorrow is another feast. Again, the attendees are limited to the king and his prime minister. Another delightful time is anticipated. One special attendee is brimming with pride. He is the only one invited!

There is one small problem: the king is suffering from insomnia. He cannot get to sleep. The text does not tell us why but highlights that fact. It does suggest, though, that this is unusual, for it specifies "on that night the king could not sleep." His predicament reminds us of the plight experienced by King Darius I, who foolishly had consigned his friend Daniel to the den of lions. Darius could not sleep either, but it was because of remorse and sorrow. To address his dilemma he "spent the night fasting; no diversions were brought to him, and sleep fled from him" (Dan. 6:18). In sharp contrast, Ahasuerus called for diversion and asked someone to read from the book of records. Not long after the reading started, the king learned about an earlier attempt on his life by two trusted doorkeepers. When discovered and documented, the traitors were promptly hanged on the gallows (2:23). To the king's disappointment and surprise, nothing had been done to reward the informant, a man by the name of Mordecai. The king knew that he had to do something. Good deeds must be rewarded.

To fully appreciate this chapter, we need to recognize that the author is employing satiric irony. Irony, says Webster's dictionary, is "the use of words to express something other than and especially the opposite of the literal meaning." On the face of it, we might be inclined to read these words as mere happenstance or coincidence. It just so happened that the king could not sleep. It just so happened that Haman was the only person in the courtyard when the king asked his question. It just so happened that both Haman and the king were focused on the same individual. As earlier stated, these seeming coincidences are, in actuality, demonstrations of divine providence. The author, God himself, controls and directs all these events to accomplish his own ends. The Ruler of nations causes insomnia, just as he plants dreams. He is the one whose Holy Spirit instills in Mordecai the desire to protect his monarch, all the while persuading him to not engage in false worship of the prime minister. The divine choreographer allows evil persons to spew out their hatred. He also controls the behavior of his saints.

We, as believers, immediately recognize the irony implicit in this scene. The wicked Haman arrives at the palace early in the morning, well before the second banquet, with one purpose. He is there to get royal permission to have this despicable Jew hung on his specially prepared gallows. He comes at the instigation of his wife, Zeresh. The king, meanwhile, is looking for someone to honor this very same Jew, one who is doubly scheduled for execution. The Judge of all the earth is probably sitting on his heavenly throne and laughing in derision. We, as readers, are also inclined to laugh. This turn of events is a literary delicacy. We know that God is going to protect his people. He has promised that since the days of Abraham, guaranteeing that "in him all the nations of the earth shall be blessed" (Gen. 12:3). Much later, the prophet Jeremiah could utter God's promise: "I will gather the remnant of my flock out of all the countries where I have driven them, and I will bring them back to their fold" (Jer. 23:3). The great plan of salvation rides on the outcome of this meeting. If Haman is allowed to live and Mordecai allowed to die, the entire Jewish populace will be in peril.

Haman's narcissism is the very thing that brings about his downfall. When the king asks his most loyal advisor how this person is to be honored, this wicked man assumes that he is to get the reward. He is the one to be honored. When Haman requests a robe that the king wore and the horse on which the king rode, he creates the impression that he wants to be the king. Thinking thus, he suggests a noble procession leading through the streets of the city. He is flabbergasted when he finds that he is to lead this procession honoring his mortal enemy. The king commands it. The king magnifies the disdain when he tells Haman to "hurry . . . and do so to Mordecai the Jew . . . and leave nothing out that you have mentioned" (6:10). Haman obeys without protest. The alternative is probable death, for the monarch demands obedience and wields the sword.

This scene gives us another glimpse into the nature of the Persian monarchy. The king is governed by the law of the Medes and the Persians, which cannot be changed, but at the same time, the king has the power and the authority to execute anyone who does not please him. He does not need a trial by jury. He does not need a judge. He simply, unequivocally, orders the death penalty. Haman cannot challenge his ruling. That kind of power is ascribed to God alone. He is the Judge of all the earth. He is the Ruler of nations.

Mordecai does not gloat. He does not plan a celebratory feast. He goes back to his post at the city gate. Haman, meanwhile, runs home to Zeresh to spill out his troubles. He tells "his friends everything that had happened to him." We expect him to focus on his troubles and the embarrassment that he has experienced. What surprises us is the response from his wise men and his wife. They respond not in anger but in fear. Their fear revolves around the possibility that Mordecai is of Jewish descent. They phrase it thus: "If Mordecai . . . is of the Jewish people, you will not overcome him but will surely fall before him" (6:13). Their question is hypothetical. It is prefaced with "if." Do these wise men not know that Mordecai is a Jew? Did they not know that King Ahasuerus had dubbed him as "the Jew" (6:10)? Did they suddenly make a connection between Mordecai, Queen Esther, the Jewish people, and Jehovah God?

The "wise men" of Persia must have had at least some dim recollections of the stupendous miracles that God had performed for his people. They should have known about Daniel being spared in the lions' den. They should have known that all of Daniel's accusers were ripped to shreds before they hit the floor of the den. They should have knowledge of King Darius's command that all residents in their own empire "are to tremble and fear before the God of Daniel, for he is the living God" (Dan. 6:24–26). They should have had some historical inkling of the ten plagues that God had sent against Egypt, and how he had drowned all of Pharaoh's army in the Red Sea. Had they "suppressed the truth in unrighteousness," thereby leaving them without excuse (Rom. 1:18–20)? Their pondering is interrupted. Eunuchs are standing at the gate, waiting to escort Haman to this second banquet that Esther had prepared.

The king shows deferential respect to Esther, addressing her as queen. Did he know that she was a close relative of Mordecai, the Jew he had just honored? Had that connection been established, or was that a closely guarded palace secret? In diplomatic doublespeak, he asks her to make both a "wish" and a "request," as though these were two different petitions. Esther politely responds with similar terminology: "let my life be granted for my wish, and my people for my request" (7:3). She, seemingly, is counting on the king's special favor, remembering that he had graciously granted her audience. She knew that he was inspired by her physical beauty. She knew that he was enamored with royal splendor. She asks what should be a most basic right, that she be allowed to live. She then adopts the king's language and follows that with a request, that her people, the Jews, be allowed to live also. She couches that request in diplomatic language, asserting that "I and my people [are] to be destroyed, to be killed, and to be annihilated" (7:4). She borrows the exact language of the royal edict, signed recently by the king (3:13). We, the readers, see this as a tacit admission that she is a Jew. She is confessing what Mordecai had commanded her not to divulge. At that moment, Esther begins to sound like Ruth the Moabitess: "Your people shall be my people, and your God my God. Where you die, I will die" (Ruth 1:16–17).

At this point the king asks a question that he should not have needed to ask: "Who is he, and where is he, who has dared to do this?" Did Ahasuerus not remember? Did he honestly not recall who had bribed him with ten thousand talents of silver (3:9) and drafted the edict? Did he not see in Haman the very evil antagonist of the Jews? Was the king so blind? So stupid as not to reflect on this edict which he had signed and approved? Esther's answer is simple and pointed: "A foe and an enemy! This wicked Haman!"

He who sits in the heavens laughs;

The Lord holds them in derision.

Then he will speak to them in his wrath,

And terrify them in his fury, saying,

As for me, I have set my King on Zion,

My holy hill. (Ps. 2:4–6)

Discussion Starters

1. What did King Ahasuerus request on the night that he could not sleep? Was that providential or coincidental? How do you know the answer to that question?

2. How soon did you catch the irony in this chapter? Did it make you laugh? Is laughter appropriate?

3. Does the silence of God imply his absence? How do you know that God is present when he is not speaking?

4. King Darius I and King Ahasuerus are both Persian monarchs. How many years had elapsed between their reigns? Would the people of Esther's time have known about Daniel and the lions' den?

5. Was there widespread hostility toward the Jews during Esther's time? What evidence can you muster?

6. Was King Ahasuerus feigning ignorance about Esther's Jewish background? Or was his ignorance genuine?

7. What was the source of Zeresh's fear of the Jews? Did the Persian people have significant knowledge about Jewish history? Did she share in her husband's anti-Semitism?

8. Do the enemies of the gospel know the truth? How do they come to know it? Do they deliberately suppress the truth in unrighteousness? Will God hold them accountable?

Chapter 7

Radical Transformations

Scripture: Esther 7:7–8:17
Background reading: 1 Samuel 15:1–9, 32–33

At the conclusion of our last lesson we saw Haman terrified before the king and queen. He has just been identified by Esther as the villain, the enemy, and the foe. As we reflect on this scene, two factors become obvious: there has again been much drinking of wine; and the king is enraged. He has a violent temper. The book of Esther revolves around a series of feasts. The menu is ignored, but the drinking of wine is emphasized. The text tells us that "the king arose in his wrath from the wine-drinking and went into the palace garden" (7:7). In each incident, the reaction of the king is one of rage or wrath. He is inclined to rash behavior.

When Esther labels Haman as the foe, the king removes to the palace gardens, not to look for evidence, not to consider his options, but to vent his anger. Upon returning to the banquet hall, he has added reason to be enraged: Haman appears to be attacking the queen. At the suggestion of one aide, he orders his own prime minister to be hung on the gallows that he, Haman, had constructed for Mordecai. This man had been his prime minister. This man had promised ten thousand talents of silver for his treasury (3:9). This is the official who had persuaded him to issue an edict allowing the annihilation of all the Jews in his empire. There is no trial. There is no search for evidence. Whatever the queen says is accepted as gospel truth. The death penalty is not enough. Confiscate all of Haman's properties and transfer them to the queen. Furthermore, take away all of Haman's authority and transfer it to Mordecai. Give him my signet ring. Give him the power to write legislation and to issue it across the empire, even without the king's endorsement or approval. Give him the authority to do whatever the king might choose to do. With the signet ring, create laws that cannot be changed or revoked.

In a society supposedly governed by the laws of the Medes and Persians, which cannot be altered, there are no defined legislative processes. The king has unlimited authority. The king can do whatever he wishes, with no restrictions, other than an inability to modify laws that are on the books. He can order executions. He can transfer property. He can make appointments. He can do all these things, even though he is progressively characterized by excessive drinking and fits of anger. He is fussy about his women, but he is also fickle regarding human rights. He has serious character flaws. The king is not a man to be emulated. He and Haman are thicker than molasses in January. They deserve each other. But the king cannot change laws once they are written.

In sharp contrast to King Ahasuerus and Haman are the characters of Esther and Mordecai. Esther presents herself as a humble, obedient servant, willing to suffer slavery without complaint. She suddenly becomes the owner of a vast estate, but she does not gloat. She does not express an interest in it per se but promptly appoints her cousin Mordecai to manage it for her. In humility and fear, Esther pleads for the lives of her fellow Jews. She confesses to the king her relationship to Mordecai (8:1) and lets him know that she, too, is a Jew. This is apparently news to the king and to Haman, even though both have labeled Mordecai as "the Jew" (3:4; 6:10; 8:7). Queen Esther becomes the savior of the Jews by identifying herself as a Jew. She pleads for her people and leans upon her personal relationship with the king as the basis for her request. "If I have found favor" becomes the ground for her plea.

Esther desires one thing, which cannot legally be granted. She asks that "an order be written to revoke the letters devised by Haman the Agagite, the son of Hammedathe, which he wrote to destroy the Jews" (8:5). What had been imperial policy suddenly becomes reduced to personal relationships. What could not be changed under any circumstances suddenly becomes as fluid as water. Esther treats the edicts not as laws of the Medes and Persians, which cannot be changed. She treats them instead as personal letters from Haman which can be revoked. Her request is for "an order be written to revoke the letters devised by Haman the Agagite" (8:5). The king, who had recently signed an edict allowing for the total annihilation of a whole population group, now suddenly grants his wife permission to "write as you please with regard to the Jews, in the name of the king, and seal it with the king's ring" (8:8). He bestows that same authority on Mordecai, suddenly treating him as though he were now the prime minister.

In connection with this sudden turn of events, the name of Haman the Agagite, the son of Hammedatha, is again introduced. This is no incidental naming of a person but a link to Israel's history. This full name is mentioned not once but six times in this short book.[1] The intent is to remind the reader of God's anger against the ancient descendants of Agag, the king of the Amalekites. Amalek, the original leader, led his people against the Israelites as they were journeying from Egypt to Canaan. In a despicable show of force, the Amalekites attacked the rear of the migration, attempting to kill off the women and children who were lagging behind (Deut. 25:17–19). Joshua was given the power to defeat them. Much later, after Saul had become king, the prophet Samuel commanded Saul to lead his army against the Amalekites and to destroy them, leaving no one alive (1 Sam. 15:1–9). God, the jealous ruler of heaven and earth,[2] is wreaking vengeance on his enemies. King Saul foolishly spared the life of Agag, their king. In his anger God removed Saul from his position as king. Samuel, the prophet, became God's executioner and hacked Agag to death (1 Sam. 15:33). Throughout Israel's history there were series of people groups who became enemies of Israel. The Moabites, the Canaanites, the Philistines, and the Assyrians come quickly to mind. The enemies of Israel are the enemies of God. They flagrantly violate God's laws and thus incur the penalty of death. Within the empire of Persia there are hundreds of thousands of people who hate the Jews and want to see them eliminated from the land. They are eager to carry out the edicts of Haman, but they need to wait until the appointed day, the thirteenth day of the twelfth month, the month Adar. God providentially controlled the rolling of the Pur (dice) so that his plan could be played out. He will protect his people. He is their God. He loves them enough to fight for them, even though they are living in sin.

Mordecai's commands must be carefully analyzed, for they are the cause of much confusion. Some commentaries become very critical of the book and claim that the Jewish people engage in revenge, which must be performed only by God himself. These critics love to cite that classic verse, "Beloved, never avenge yourselves, but leave it to the wrath of God, for it is written,

'Vengeance is mine, I will repay, say the Lord" (Rom. 12:19). That verse, of course, stands, but it does not apply to the book of Esther. Mordecai does not demand the right to exercise revenge. His new executive order "allowed the Jews to gather and defend their lives, to destroy, to kill, and to annihilate any armed force of any people or province that might attack them, children and women included, and to plunder their goods" (8:11). The basic language is borrowed verbatim from the edicts issued by Haman. In simple language, the Jews have the right to gather or organize themselves into militia, armed squadrons, or military units. They have the right to defend themselves, even to the point of killing their enemies who are attacking them. That is not revenge. That is self-defense.

To understand the historical context correctly, the reader needs to recall the level of hostility experienced by the Jewish people. Looking back, they could recall the proclamations recently posted all over the empire that allowed the Persian people to "destroy, to kill, and to annihilate" any Jew that they found, for no reason other than their being a Jew. That edict had caused them tremendous grief and sorrow. Under Haman's orders, they had no defense. They had no right to protect self or property. They were despised slaves, as Ezra (Ezra 9:9) and Nehemiah (9:36) so graphically point out some years later. As slaves, they had no police protection and no military might. They were scheduled for extermination. Those edicts bear striking similarities to the laws promulgated by Hitler during the 1930s in Germany. The Nazis were the enemies of God's people and thus were enemies of God. Haman, the Agagite, is a precursor of Hitler. God ordered his death and used a prophet to carry it out.

If we look back into the time when Darius I was king of Persia, we read into the story of Daniel and the lions' den an implied hatred of the Jews, focused on their leader Daniel. Daniel is destined for death, not because he had done wrong, but because King Cyrus had given such incredible amounts of gold and silver to the Jews who chose to return to Jerusalem at the conclusion of the seventy years. In addition, Cyrus had given them extensive legislative, taxing, and judicial privileges (Ezra 2:64–69; 6:8–11). The Persian people had been forced to pay taxes for the rebuilding of the temple in Jerusalem and to pay the salaries of the Jewish clergy. They even had to pay for the animals used for sacrifices. Quite naturally, these idol worshippers resisted and resented such. That deep-seated tension had also resulted in a work stoppage on the temple for ten years (Ezra 6:13–18).

The greatest transformation comes to Mordecai. Three short months prior he had lain in sackcloth and ashes, crying out in loud and bitter wails. He was devastated; he anticipated genocide for his countrymen. Then, unexpectedly, he is paraded through the capital streets on the king's horse, dressed in robes worn by the king. He is heralded as the one whom the king desires to honor. Now, because of Esther's impassioned plea, he is given the king's signet ring. He is given "royal robes of blue and white, with a great golden crown" on his head. He suddenly becomes royalty, with delirious crowds shouting his praises. In an ultimate form of compliment, "many from the peoples of the country declared themselves Jews, for fear of the Jews had fallen on them" (8:17).

As we will see in the next chapter, Mordecai's new edicts allowed for the deaths of thousands upon thousands of enemies. The Jewish defense forces were highly successful, and Mordecai became the most powerful man in the Persian Empire. The celebration of the Feast of Purim was mandated for year after year, without exception. Neither Ezra nor Nehemiah makes mention of this horrific conflict, but each one informs us of continuing hostility against the Jews during their day. Nehemiah records the conflicts which erupted when they tried to rebuild the walls of Jerusalem, which had lain demolished for 141 years. Ezra informs us about the Samaritans who harassed the returning remnant.

Discussion Starters

1. How does King Ahasuerus conduct himself when Esther identifies Haman as "the enemy"? Is that rational behavior? Or, would you consider that irrational?

2. Is the author of Esther presenting facts, or is he engaging in character development to fit the story line?

3. Is Haman given a fair trial? Does he deserve to be hanged on his own gallows?

4. Did Haman have an extensive estate? What evidence can you submit for your conclusion?

5. Esther informs the king that Mordecai is her cousin and that she, therefore, is a Jew. What impact did that have on the king?

6. What is the difference between the legislation that Mordecai drafted and that drafted by Haman? Why is some of the language identical?

7. Is it fair to accuse Esther and Mordecai of revenge? Is there some sense in which this is God's revenge against the Amalekites for their attacks against the Israelites many centuries before?

8. How would you explain the fact that many Persians suddenly called themselves Jews? Can you think of any parallel situations in history?

Notes

1. The name appears in Esther 3:1, 10; 8:3, 5; 9:10, 24.
2. God identifies himself as jealous (Exod. 20:5; 34:14). Jealousy, best understood as a deep-seated protective attitude toward one's own people, is an attribute and name of God, self-imposed.

Chapter 8

An Unbalanced Civil War

Scripture: Esther 9–10
Background reading: Exodus 12:1–6

A Scripted Conflict

As we open Esther 9, we ought to scratch our heads over the highly unusual sequence of events. In the previous chapter we noted that royal edicts had gone out to all of the 127 provinces of this vast empire. Two royal edicts, both signed by King Ahasuerus, have been posted in multiple languages in every city and village of these many provinces. The first edict permitted Persian citizens to kill, destroy, and annihilate any person of Jewish descent, and to confiscate all of their possessions. The second edict permitted all Jewish persons to organize into military units and to defend themselves against any person who might attack them. The king has given full approval to civil war within his empire.

What is ironic is the fact that this civil war may not start until the thirteenth day of the twelfth month and may last for only one day. In almost comic fashion, this war is being orchestrated as though it were intended to settle a long-standing feud between two opposing parties. There is obviously deep-seated hatred against the Jewish population, for the words "enemies" and "hatred" occur multiple times in the chapter. There is a defined element within the Persian population that despises all Jews and wants them executed. Some commentaries suggest that these are Amalekites connected with Haman's family. The connection with Haman is beyond dispute, but the text does not offer definitive evidence as to the identity of these enemies. The choice of starting date for the conflict is also connected with Haman, who superstitiously wanted to organize this genocide. This casting of the lot was reported in Esther 3:7, which happened in the month Nisan.[1] That, coincidentally, was also the month of the Passover, which was specified by God. The roll of the Pur was apparently controlled by God, who had his own agenda in mind. The setting of that date allowed the Jews ample time to organize their defenses, but it also restricted their enemies in their attacks. The chatter in the villages must have approached that date with intense fear and trepidation.

When the thirteenth day of the twelfth month arrived, the balance of power had radically shifted. "All the officials of the provinces and the satraps and the governors and the royal agents helped the Jews, for the fear of Mordecai had fallen on them" (9:3). The rapid rise to power by Mordecai is highly unusual and can be attributed only to the blessing of God. It is not uncommon for government officials to rally around their king or prime minister in times of national danger, but for such to occur within the space of one year is unique. But it is not only the monarch who attracts support. The Jewish people themselves "gained mastery over those who hated them" (9:2).

The Casualty Count

The Jews were restricted to defensive measures. They might only fight and kill those persons who attacked them. On that first day of conflict, they killed five hundred men in the citadel of Susa. Then, almost parenthetically, the king adds the names of Haman's ten sons.

Susa is the seat of imperial government. That is the capitol of the empire. The king, almost nonchalantly, informs the queen of the body count, expressing neither regret nor alarm. Treating her almost as field marshal, he inquires of her as to the casualty count in the rest of the empire. Before she responds to his request, she asks for two more favors: may we extend the edict for one more day in Susa, and may we have the bodies of the ten slain sons of Haman hanged on the gallows where he had been hung? The king immediately grants her wishes and commands those bodies to be hanged for all to see. Her request applies only to the capital city and not to the rest of the empire. The text gives no rationale for that narrow request, but its significance should not be lost on the reader. The implication is that there is an additional concentration of enemies in the capital city. The double date for defense will also send a clear message to the ruling party, headquartered in Susa. King Ahasuerus should be profoundly impressed when the God of the Hebrews protects his people, without any of them falling in battle. When we project ahead to the books of Ezra and Nehemiah, there seems to be an intense desire on the part of King Artaxerxes to promote and protect the worship of Jehovah.[2]

The next day there are an additional 300 deaths in the capital city. In comparison with the rest of the empire, that body count is relatively small, but significant nonetheless. In one day, the Jews were able to kill 75,000 of their enemies, without losing any of their own men in battle (9:16). Such numbers often become the object of ridicule, with critics implying that the author of this book was obviously engaging in hyperbole and fabrication. The faithful follower of God will not buy into such assessment, for the Bible frequently reports such unusual numbers. When the king of Assyria threatened to destroy Jerusalem and capture King Hezekiah, God put to death 185,000 soldiers in one night as they camped around the city (Isa. 37:36). When the Lord pronounced judgment on one of David's sins, he sent a pestilence on Israel, which killed 70,000 men in one day (2 Sam. 24:15). When God opened the Red Sea for Israel to walk through on dry ground, he allowed Pharaoh's army to follow them in and then let the waters return to their normal levels, drowning the entire army (Exod. 14:28).

The Creator of heaven and earth is an awesome God, able to give life but also to decree death. As we have stated before, the warfare etched on the pages of Esther is ultimately a battle between God and Satan, between good and evil, between God's children and his enemies. Similar numbers of casualties are reported throughout the Bible, reminding us of his justice and his power. The penalty for enmity against the Sovereign is death. It is here being demonstrated in Persia.

The original edict allowing the Persians permission to "destroy, to kill, and to annihilate" the Jews also gave them permission "to plunder their goods." That same privilege was granted to the Jews in the edict granting them the right to defend themselves. Of significance is the fact that the Jews never once plundered the goods of their enemies. That behavior set them apart and demonstrated that they were not desirous of becoming wealthy. Their only purpose was in preserving their lives. Even though they were surrounded by enemies who genuinely hated them, they did not crave their goods or deny their wives and children the basic necessities of life. The Jews were God's chosen people and acted in compliance with his tenth commandment: "thou shalt not covet." Their behavior was exemplary and may help to explain why "many from the peoples of the country declared themselves Jews" (8:17).

The Commands to Celebrate

When the two days of slaughter were accomplished, Mordecai, as prime minister of the empire, sent letters to all the Jews in all the provinces, "obliging them to keep the fourteenth day of the month Adar and also the fifteenth day of the same, year by year," as a national holiday (9:21). Upon receipt of these letters, "the Jews firmly obligated themselves and their offspring and all who joined them" (9:27). They further resolved "that these days should be remembered and kept throughout every generation in every clan, province, and city, and that these days of Purim should never fall into disuse" (9:28).

We, as students of Scripture, should wonder if those pledges and promises were kept. Did the Jewish people repeatedly celebrate the Feast of Purim? Did the remnant, by now settled in Judea, ever celebrate this feast? We also need to question whether this command from Mordecai had the blessing and endorsement from Jehovah. Did God in any way confirm or establish such an annual celebration?

The Feast of Purim, or the Feast of Passover?

Many years before the events recorded for us in the book of Esther, there was a large-scale migration of Jews back to Jerusalem. That migration occurred in the year 538 BC and was made possible by the commands of King Cyrus, the first ruler of Persia. That event is recorded for us in 2 Chronicles 36:22—23 and in Ezra 1–2. That return from exile had been promised by God in Jeremiah 29:10–14 and in Isaiah 44–45. Ezra, the outstanding, well-qualified historian, records those events in chapters 1 through 6. He describes that return from exile and reminds us that those returning peoples were anxious to worship God precisely as he had commanded in the law. Ezra also informs us that the returned exiles kept the Passover on the fourteenth day of the first month (Ezra 6:19), the same year that the rebuilt temple was dedicated in 515 BC. That turns out to be the same calendar day that Mordecai would later command the Jews to celebrate the Feast of Purim. Did Mordecai recognize the conflict? Did Mordecai and all the Jews who promised to obey his commands not know about Exodus 12 and God's commands to celebrate the Passover on the fourteenth day of the first month?

God used the Passover as the tenth plague against Pharaoh as a final, convincing act to force the Egyptian peoples to let Israel leave their land. The Passover had two dimensions to it. On the one hand, it promised life to God's people. On the other hand, it resulted in death for God's enemies. God then commanded Israel to celebrate Passover every year on the fourteenth day of the first month as a memorial to their release from slavery. Now, more than one thousand years later, Mordecai seems to be ignoring the Passover and substitutes the Feast of Purim as the Jews escape from death. He initiates a secular holiday where there should have been a spiritual memorial service.

Esther becomes queen of Persia in the year 479 BC. That is only thirty-six years after the temple was rebuilt and dedicated in Jerusalem. Twenty-one years after Esther becomes queen, King Artaxerxes commissions Ezra to go to Jerusalem for the express purpose of "making inquiries about Judah and Jerusalem according to the Law of your God, which is in your hand" (Ezra 7:14). This was not a personal desire of the king but a decision "by the king and his seven counselors." The proper worship of Jehovah was a national priority.

A Continuing Mystery

When we take historical chronology seriously, we are left with a mystery that has no easy answers. The events of Esther obviously precede the books of Ezra, Nehemiah, and Malachi. All three of those authors lived during the time that Esther was queen and Mordecai was prime minister. All of them must have been familiar with the Feast of Purim, for it was required every year among all of the Jewish population. Yet, surprisingly, none of these three authors makes even oblique references to Esther, to Mordecai, or to Purim. The book of Ezra, in fact, seems to avoid that era of Jewish history. As a historian, Ezra devotes chapters 1 through 6 to the events that occurred between 539 BC and 515 BC. He focuses not on Susa but on Jerusalem, not on military threats but on religious observances. True to his calling, he emphasizes the importance of worshipping God as it was prescribed in Mosaic law. Then, when he gets to Ezra 7, Ezra shifts to reporting on his own commissioning by King Artaxerxes. He leapfrogs from 515 BC to 458 BC, a span of fifty-seven years, omitting the era of Esther and Mordecai. Why? Is Ezra perhaps making a statement about the evils of cultural accommodation by ignoring it? When Nehemiah follows thirteen years later, he, too, focuses on Jerusalem and worship, ignoring the events in the rest of the empire. Is God, the primary author of Scripture, directing his writers to shift from secular society in Susa to religious observances in Jerusalem? Is God calling his people to repentance? Without clear textual evidence, that appears to be the case.

Discussion Starters

1. Do civil wars usually start on a specific date, prescribed in advance? Why did Haman choose the thirteenth day of the twelfth month?

2. Do you believe that God was controlling the roll of the Pur? If yes, why would God pick the date that he did?

3. Why would a sizable portion of Persia's population hate the Jews and wish them killed? Read Ezra 6:6–12 for answers.

4. Did the Jews kill women and children on the day that was assigned? Would their enemies have killed women and children if they could have?

5. Why did the Jews refrain from taking any plunder when they had opportunity?

6. Should the Jews have celebrated Passover instead of the Feast of Purim? Why? What are some of the differences between these two feasts?

7. Why do Ezra, Nehemiah, and Malachi ignore or fail to mention Esther, Mordecai, or Purim?

8. How would you justify Esther as part of Scripture when some reject its inclusion?

9. What lessons can we learn from our study of Esther? Would you recommend it for study by new converts? Why not?

Notes

1. Exodus 12:1–2. The Hebrew name for that month was Abib, but the Babylonian name was Nisan.
2. See Ezra 7:1–6, 13–16; Nehemiah 2:4–9.

Note to the Reader

The publisher invites you to respond to us about this book by writing to Reformed Fellowship, Inc., at *president@reformedfellowship.net*

Founded in 1951, Reformed Fellowship, Inc., is a religious and strictly nonprofit organization composed of a group of Christian believers who hold to the biblical Reformed faith. Our purpose is to advocate and propagate this faith, to nurture those who seek to live in obedience to it, to give sharpened expression to it, to stimulate the doctrinal sensitivities of those who profess it, to promote the spiritual welfare and purity of the Reformed churches, and to encourage Christian action.

Members of Reformed Fellowship express their adherence to the Calvinistic creeds as formulated in the *Belgic Confession*, the *Heidelberg Catechism*, the *Canons of Dort*, and the *Westminster Confession and Catechisms*.

To fulfill our mission, we publish a bimonthly journal, *The Outlook*, and we publish books and Bible study guides. Our website is *www.reformedfellowship.net*.

MORE BIBLE STUDY MATERIALS AVAILABLE FROM REFORMED FELLOWSHIP!

Purchase online at www.reformedfellowship.net
or email: sales@reformedfellowship.net

Amos Bible Studies
Rev. Henry Vander Kam
Paperback, 96 pages

Daniel Bible Studies
Rev. John Piersma
Paperback, 80 pages

Genesis 1-11 Bible Studies
Rev. Mark Vander Hart
Paperback, 186 pages

The Gospel-Driven Tongue: Lessons from James on Godly Conversation
Rev. Brian G. Najapfour
Paperback, 72 pages

Gospel Power Magnified through Human Weakness (2 Corinthians)
Dr. Nelson Kloosterman
Paperback, 101 pages

Jacob Bible Studies
Rev. Mark Vander Hart
Paperback, 156 pages

Joseph & Judah Bible Studies
Rev. Mark Vander Hart
Paperback, 80 pages

Letter to the Ephesians
Rev. Henry Vander Kam
Paperback, 132 pages

Meeting Jesus at the Feast: Israel's Festivals and the Gospel
Dr. John R. Sittema
Paperback, 160 pages

1 Peter Bible Studies
Rev. Henry Vander Kam
Paperback, 165 pages

Ruth Bible Studies
Dr. L. Charles Jackson
Paperback, 176 pages

1 & 2 Thessalonians Bible Studies
Rev. Henry Vander Kam
Paperback, 136 pages

1 Timothy Bible Studies
Rev. Henry Vander Kam
Paperback, 112 pages

2 Timothy & Titus Bible Studies
Rev. Henry Vander Kam
Paperback, 100 pages

The Law of the Lord as Our Delight (Deuteronomy)
Dr. Nelson Kloosterman
Paperback, 100 pages

The Parables of Our Lord
Rev. Henry Vander Kam
Paperback, 66 pages

Bible Studies on Mark
Rev William Boekestein
Paperback, 212 pages

LIFE IN CHRIST CATECHISM SERIES:

Not My Own
by Glenda Mathes
Intermediate (Grades 5 and 6)
Spiral bound, 168 pages

God's Unfolding Promise
by Laurie Vanden Heuvel
Intermediate (Grades 5 and 6)
Spiral bound, 216 pages

Christ's Living Church
by Rev. Ronald Scheuers
Middle School (Grades 7 and 8)
Spiral bound, 232 pages

Faith of Our Fathers
by Revs. Bradd L. Nymeyer and Al Bezuyen
Middle School (Grades 7 and 8)
Spiral bound, 200 pages

The Price of Possession 1
by Dr. Warren H. Lammers
High School (Grades 9 through 12)
Spiral bound, 232 pages

The Price of Possession 2
by Dr. Warren H. Lammers
High School (Grades 9 through 12)
Spiral bound, 232 pages

The Doctrines of Grace
by Revs. John A. Bouwers and Ronald L. Scheuers
High School (Grades 9 through 12)
Spiral bound, 232 pages

Facing Faith's Challenges
by Rev. Andrew A. Cammenga
High School (Grades 9 through 12)
Spiral bound, 208 pages

Notes